I want to be a Firefighter

Other titles in this series:

I want to be a Cowboy
I want to be a Pilot

I WANT TO BE A

Firefighter

FIREFLY BOOKS

A FIREFLY BOOK

Published by Firefly Books Ltd. 1999

First Printing

Library of Congress Cataloging-in-Publication Data is available.

Canadian Cataloguing in Publication Data

Main entry under title:

I want to be a firefighter

ISBN 1-55209-448-0 (bound)
ISBN 1-55209-433-2 (pbk.)

1. Fire extinction – Juvenile literature.   2. Fire fighters – Juvenile literature.

| TH9148/I25 | 1999 | j363.37 | C99-930932-3 |

Published in Canada in 1999 by
Firefly Books Ltd.
3680 Victoria Park Avenue
Willowdale, Ontario, Canada M2H 3K1

Published in the United States in 1999 by
Firefly Books (U.S.) Inc.
P.O. Box 1338, Ellicott Station
Buffalo, New York, USA 14205

Design by Interrobang Graphic Design Inc.
Printed and bound in Canada by Kromar, Winnipeg, Manitoba

The Publisher acknowledges the financial support of the Government of Canada through the Book Publishing Industry Development Program for its publishing activities.

Firefighters must come to the rescue quickly when there is a fire. They drive trucks called fire engines.

The fire engine carries a powerful hose and a long ladder. It has a siren to use when there is a fire. Have you heard the noise fire engines make?

Firefighters must be strong to carry the heavy equipment and control the powerful fire hoses.

The hose sprays water into the middle of the flames. The firefighters must hold on tightly!

Fires can happen at any time. Sometimes firefighters must work all night.

The smoke from a fire can make people sick, so firefighters carry tanks of fresh air to breathe.

This firefighter is trying to put out flames on a roof. He doesn't want the building to burn down. Do you think he will put out the fire in time?

Firefighters make sure everyone is safe. Sometimes firefighters are hurt while helping other people.

Sometimes cars catch fire. Although the fire is small, these firefighters are careful to protect their bodies with thick coats.

Look at all the controls on this fire truck! The firefighter knows what each one is for.

When there are no fires, firefighters wait at the firehouse. They make sure their equipment is clean and works properly.

This fire was hard to reach from the ground, so the firefighter sprays water down on it from high above.

Sometimes fires start on boats or ships, or on buildings near the water. Fireboat to the rescue!

Helicopters can dump water over large areas. That's important because forest fires spread quickly.

Small towns use volunteer firefighters. They may be cooks, dentists or librarians, but they all come running when the town siren wails.

This man knew he wanted to be a firefighter when he was a small boy. He is very tired, but he always feels glad that he is helping people.